The Beginner's Guide to Basic Credit Management

L. CRAIG TAYLOR

The Beginner's Guide to Basic Credit Management

A Biblical Perspective

MDP PUBLICATIONS

Greenwood, Indiana 46143

www.mdp-publications.com

The Beginner's Guide to Basic Credit Management

L. Craig Taylor

Copyright ©2003 by L. Craig Taylor

Published by **MDP PUBLICATIONS**

Greenwood, IN 46143

Cover design by L. Craig Taylor

Graphics and Clip-Art Copyright ©2001 Microsoft Corporation

All scripture quotations in this publication are from the *King James Version* of the Bible unless otherwise identified.

MDP PUBLICATIONS

www.mdp-publications.com

Substantial discounts on bulk quantities of this book are available. For details and discount information, please visit our website or contact our special sales department: *specialsales@mdp-publications.com*

ISBN: 0-9741335-0-7

Library of Congress Control Number: 2003106353

Printed in the United States of America
by Moeller Printing Co., Indianapolis, Indiana

First printing: May 2003
10 9 8 7 6 5 4 3 2 1

For Carly, Geneva Ruth, and Joseph David
I love you all!

Always remember:
Desire makes a way; lack of desire makes an excuse!

Table of Contents

Acknowledgments

Thank you, Jesus, for being so merciful to me. You have blessed me more than I deserve! Your grace is *amazing*.

A very special thank you to my wife for putting up with me while I worked on this project. Thanks for all the advice and the time you spent looking over my shoulder. I love you.

Also, a sincere thanks to Rev. O.C. Marler and Rev. Tom O'Daniel for encouraging me to go forward with this project and for providing insight and advice along the way.

Thanks to all those who read the advanced copies and offered your opinions, suggestions, and endorsements. Thanks to Yvette Cunningham for proofreading this project for me. Thanks to Dawn Sipes for the information that you provided.

Thanks to Bro. Tom Butler, my mentor and friend. You will probably never realize the influence that you have had on me.

Thanks to my dear friends, Alva and Okie Deaton, for your prayers and encouragement. You exemplify good stewardship.

Thanks to my parents for believing in me. Thanks to my Grandmother, Jerlene Elledge. You have been my rock, and without your prayers this would not have been possible.

Although he has already gone on to be with his Lord, I must also thank my late Grandfather, Rev. O.S. Elledge, who taught me the value of managing wisely when I was young. His example of stewardship and his sound advice will always affect me, and I hope his memory will be honored by this project.

Forward

The world of credit has changed ever so dramatically over the past several years. Today's evolving and expanding credit options easily entice the unwary down a path to financial bondage. Financial institutions now offer a myriad of installment loan types, interest rate options, equity reserve accounts, and credit cards that offer an endless variety of fees, rates, terms, and payments. Ultimately, they bind the unsuspecting into financial slavery as individuals sell out to the system of the world in order to enjoy present wants at the expense of future needs.

The disturbing trend of increased financial bondage should concern the child of God. All Christians will choose, consciously or by default, to operate under God's authority or the world's authority regarding financial management. The Lord liberates, frees the soul, and desires that none be in bondage; however, many yield to the worldly system and lose themselves in credit, which potentially allows them to fall under financial oppression. The taskmasters of bill collectors and wage garnishers sabotage every paycheck. The innocent find themselves seduced into situations that make it nearly impossible to align themselves with the Godly principles of tithing and giving. Thus, they fail to live under God's covenant of protection and cannot enter into the blessed life that Jesus promised on earth: *"But he shall receive an hundredfold now in this time, houses, and brethren, and sisters, and mothers, and children, and lands, with persecutions; and in the world to come eternal life." (Mark 10:30)*

> **MONEY MANAGEMENT REFLECTS THE INNER PERSON AND SPEAKS OF THE ISSUES OF THE HEART.**

In this work, Craig Taylor has done an excellent job of outlining the basics of credit management and advised how to avoid the pitfalls that will ensnare the uninformed. He details how to shun the credit trap and evade financial bondage. Brother Taylor's advice within the pages of this book will prove to be a vital weapon in the Christian arsenal to fight and maintain freedom. Ultimately, he provides tools and principles that can aid us in achieving an overcoming life.

Money management reflects the inner person and speaks of the issues of the heart. Wise disciples of Jesus carefully structure and manage their finances and thereby demonstrate Christ's control of the soul. Therefore, read, grasp, and apply these principles; submit your inner person to Jesus and reap the temporal and eternal benefits of Biblical financial stewardship. Place *The Beginner's Guide to Basic Credit Management* into your library as a resource for your life, and build its principles into your soul to govern your daily decisions.

Thank you, Brother Taylor, for your outstanding work that promises to serve every reader with sound life principles and produce innumerable blessings.

–Thomas A. Butler, CFP, CLU, ChFC

$\mathcal{I}$ntroduction

$\mathcal{M}$oney is a very important part of our lives. Effectively managing it can help to eliminate stress and anxiety, and it can help to bring us peace of mind. So many people desire to manage their personal finances more effectively, but they just do not know where to start.

On a recent trip to the library to do research for this project, I was amazed by the number of books on the topic of managing your money. It was almost overwhelming. There were rows and rows of books on almost every conceivable aspect of finances. I can certainly understand how someone with no experience at all would be discouraged and give up before they even get started. That is why I felt it important to put this information together. I wanted to produce something simple and straightforward to assist people in beginning on the right foot.

Beginning on the wrong foot can be financial suicide. According to the American Bankruptcy Institute, there were 1,217,972 consumer bankruptcy filings in America in the year 2000. Poor money management can cause other problems as well. Statistics reveal that

> **STATISTICS REVEAL THAT IN 85-90% OF ALL DIVORCES, FINANCIAL DIFFICULTY IS CITED AS A CONTRIBUTING FACTOR.**

in 85 to 90 percent of all divorces, financial difficulty is cited as a contributing factor. Additionally, losing control of your finances can cause stress and anxiety that may contribute to poor health and spiritual problems.

Many of these problems are a result of poor credit management. Knowing how to manage your credit wisely can be a great benefit to you. Avoiding common mistakes and pitfalls can save you thousands of dollars and eliminate needless worry and stress from your life.

Wise credit management is an integral part of good stewardship. The Bible has plenty to say about stewardship. Perhaps the best-known reference is the parable of the talents found in Matthew 25:14-30. From this parable, it is clear that we are expected to administer wisely the things that God has given to us. 1 Corinthians 4:2 states, *"Moreover it is required in stewards that a man be found faithful."*

I will never forget the very first lesson in our Ministerial Finance class at Indiana Bible College. The instructor, Thomas Butler, stressed to us the fact that "stewardship implies no ownership." We are to be good stewards over the things that God has placed in our trust. Obviously, this applies to our lives and our character as well as our finances. Everything belongs to God. We do not own anything. The Psalmist said it this way in Psalms 24:1, *"The earth is the Lord's, and the fulness thereof; the world, and they that dwell therein."* Haggai 2:8 says, *"The silver is mine, and the gold is mine, saith the*

Lord of hosts." Since it all belongs to God and we are only taking care of what is His, we must be very careful not to overlook our responsibilities.

Considering the fact that everything we have comes from God, it is interesting how easily we justify all of the ways

> **"STEWARDSHIP IMPLIES NO OWNERSHIP."**
> -Thomas A. Butler

that we mismanage. Not only do we often mismanage, but we also frequently fail to give back to the kingdom of God as we should. One of the most common excuses people give for not tithing is, "I cannot afford it!" The heavy burden of debt that is created by poor credit management is often the basis for this feeling. This is not God's plan. We should live free from unnecessary and unreasonable debt so that we can serve God with everything we have; it all belongs to Him.

The Biblical model is for us to give to the Kingdom of God *first*. It has never been God's plan for us to be so far in debt that we cannot give our tithes and offerings. It has never been His plan for us to spend everything that we make before giving back to Him.

Malachi 3:8-10 gives us some interesting and powerful insight into this issue:

> *"⁸Will a man rob God? Yet ye have robbed me. But ye say, Wherein have we robbed thee? In tithes and offerings. ⁹Ye are cursed with a curse: for ye have robbed me, even this whole nation. ¹⁰Bring ye all the tithes into the storehouse, that there may be meat in mine house, and prove me now herewith, saith the Lord of hosts, if I will not open you the*

windows of heaven, and pour you out a blessing, that there shall not be room enough to receive it."

Notice verse nine, *"Ye are cursed with a curse: for ye have robbed me."* By not tithing and giving their offerings, Israel had incurred a curse from God! This important fact should not be overlooked. You will never help yourself by failing to give God what rightfully belongs to Him. If you fail to tithe because you "can't afford it," your situation may become even worse. Make up your mind to be a faithful tither. *Always* **give God what belongs to Him.** By doing so, you can turn a curse into a blessing.

> ## MAKE UP YOUR MIND TO BE A FAITHFUL TITHER.

The New American Standard Version of the Bible translates verse ten this way, *"'Bring the whole tithe into the storehouse, so that there may be food in My house, and test Me now in this,' says the Lord of Hosts, 'if I will not open for you the windows of heaven, and pour out for you a blessing until there is no more need.'"*

Larry Burkett made this comment regarding the passage:

> This is the only place in Scripture where God ever told His people to test Him. Plus this passage makes the principle of the tithe clear. It's an outside indicator of an inside spiritual condition. It's our testimony that God owns everything in our lives.[1]

---

[1] Larry Burkett, Answers to Your Family's Financial Questions (Pomona, CA: Focus on the Family Publishing, 1987) 107

It is clear that we are expected to bring our tithes and offerings into the storehouse. Not only does this keep us from robbing God, but it also demonstrates that we are completely surrendered to Him. Additionally, our obedience makes us eligible to reap the benefits of God's promised blessings.

Dr. John MacArthur said the following:

> To underscore how important the subject of money and possessions is to God, sixteen of Christ's thirty-eight parables speak about how people should handle earthly treasure. In fact, our Lord taught more about stewardship (one out of every ten verses in the Gospels) than about heaven and hell combined. The entire Bible contains more than two thousand references to wealth and property, twice as many as the total references to faith and prayer. What we do with the *things* God has given us is very important to Him.[2]

I have compiled this information to benefit young adults, young couples, and others who need to understand the basics of credit management. I trust that putting God first, being faithful in your tithes and offerings, and following these simple guidelines will help you discover the peace that comes from being in control of your finances and managing your credit wisely.

An Important Note to the Reader: The Glossary contains some very important, detailed information regarding many of the terms and concepts referred to in this guide. I recommend that you read through it initially and then refer to it as necessary while you read.

---

[2]John F. MacArthur, Jr., *Whose Money Is It Anyway? A Biblical Guide to Using God's Wealth* (Nashville: Word, 2000) 3.

Credit Management

Credit can be a great friend or a terrible enemy; it all depends on how you manage it. Used properly, credit can be a great asset in many ways. Having the ability to borrow money can allow you to buy a home, purchase a vehicle, or start your own business. However, being too far in debt and not properly managing your credit can have devastating effects. Managing your credit may often make you feel like you are walking a tightrope.

> **CREDIT CAN BE A GREAT FRIEND OR A TERRIBLE ENEMY; IT ALL DEPENDS ON HOW YOU MANAGE IT.**

In this guide we will take a look at some things you should know about credit. We will look at what the Bible says about borrowing money and our scriptural responsibilities. We will also look at some of the advantages and disadvantages of credit cards and consumer loans. Finally, we will take a brief look at some of your options concerning auto loans and home mortgages.

Case Study I

Mary is a sophomore at a private college. She is friendly, popular, has many friends, and is known to be a very responsible person. Most of the people who know her think that she has the potential to be anything she wants to be. Mary is known as a "sharp dresser" and always keeps up with the latest styles and fashions in clothing. Until recently, Mary has always been an "A" and "B" student; but her grades have started to slip in the most recent semester.

Soon after she moved into her dorm, she began receiving offers for "pre-approved" credit cards. Mary applied and was approved for three of them in her first semester at college. The credit limits are $1,500, $2,000, and $2,500. She was very excited to receive the credit cards, and being approved for them reinforced her belief that she was now a responsible adult. She promised herself that she would only use them in emergencies or for pre-planned expenses.

Wendy and Susie are Mary's best friends. Their parents are wealthy, and they always have the best of everything. The purchasing power of the credit cards helps Mary to "fit in" a little better when she shops with her friends. Without the credit cards, she would not be able to keep up with the latest fashions; she might not be cool enough to hang out with Wendy and Susie. She has "maxed out" two of the cards and only has about $500 of available credit on the third.

Mary works part-time but is struggling to pay her car payment, insurance, tuition, and credit card bills. The credit card bills are way behind, and Mary has stopped answering her phone because the collection agencies keep calling. She feels that they should understand that she is a college student and thinks they will eventually give up if she doesn't answer their calls. She has been working some overtime lately to make extra money, and her grades are starting to suffer. She is also behind on her tuition, and her car payment is due in two weeks. Mary is afraid that she will not be able to pay it.

Mary has applied for a job as a bank teller. The pay is better, and the bank will reimburse her college tuition. She feels that it would allow her to catch up on her overdue accounts. Mary has completed two interviews, and the manager is very impressed with her. She has been told she will get the job if her credit report is satisfactory.

The bank just called and informed Mary that her credit report will not allow them to hire her. She is frustrated and feels that she will have to drop out of college. Mary doesn't want to lose her car, but she cannot pay her tuition and other payments also. The bill collectors won't stop calling and are now threatening legal action. Mary is angry and feels that the credit card company is to blame for her problems because they issued the cards to her when she could not afford them.

THE BIBLE AND CREDIT

What does the Bible say about borrowing money and being in debt? As an answer, many people will quote the following "verse": *"Neither a borrower nor a lender be."* The truth of the matter is that this "verse" comes from Benjamin Franklin's *Poor Richard's Almanac;* it is not from the Bible at all.

Romans 13:8 *is* in the Bible and it says, *"Owe no man any thing . . . "* This verse is often quoted by those who believe the Bible teaches against borrowing money. Is that really what this scripture is referring to? Unfortunately, they often fail to finish the verse, *". . . but to love one another: for he that loveth another hath fulfilled the law."* The scripture immediately before that says, *"Render therefore to all their dues: tribute to whom tribute is due; custom to whom custom; fear to whom fear; honor to whom honor." (Romans 13:7)* Most scholars agree that Paul was not forbidding us from borrowing money in verse eight. Also, there are many other scriptures in the Bible that deal with borrowing and lending money. If Paul would have been talking about that, I think he would have made it very clear. However, we *are* obligated to responsibly repay what we owe so that we do not harm others.

Having said that, the Bible does provide us with principles related to borrowing. Psalms 37:21 says, *"The wicked borroweth, and payeth not again: but the righteous sheweth mercy, and giveth."* The implication in this verse is clear—if we borrow from someone, then we are supposed to repay them. If we do not, then we are considered wicked.

Proverbs 22:7 also warns us about borrowing. It says, *"The rich ruleth over the poor, and the borrower is servant to the lender."* When we borrow money we are obligated to the person or company that we

> **"THE RICH RULETH OVER THE POOR, AND THE BORROWER IS SERVANT TO THE LENDER."**
> *(PROVERBS 22:7)*

borrow it from.   During Bible times there were very strict penalties for not repaying what you owed.

You may remember the story in 2 Kings 4:1-7 about the widow who came to the prophet Elisha. She was distraught because her husband had died and she was unable to pay their debts. She told the prophet that the creditors were going to come and take her sons away from her and make them slaves if she did not repay the debts. Fortunately, God miraculously intervened for her; and she was able to repay the debts before her sons were taken away.

If people did not repay their debts, they were sold into slavery or thrown into prison. Thankfully, we do not throw people into prison or force them into slavery today the way they did then. In spite of that, we are still supposed to honor our commitments and repay our debts. This is a Biblical principle.

Hebrews 13:5 teaches us, *"Let your conversation be without covetousness; and be content with such things as ye have."* If we are using credit for the purpose of keeping up with someone else or to satisfy all of our material wants and desires, then it will probably lead us into trouble and heartache. (Remember Mary in our Case Study?) That is not God's purpose for our lives. He does not want us to be slaves to this world or its system.

The more money you owe, the more money you will have to earn to repay your debts and fulfill your obligations. Although there is nothing wrong with having nice things, we must ask ourselves what price we are willing to pay. Possessions do not make us happy.

Many families have been destroyed because of financial problems. As I mentioned in the introduction, statistics reveal that 85 to 90 percent of all divorcing couples cite financial difficulties as a contributing factor. Although there are many specific reasons for this, one is the tremendous pressure that is created by being deeply in debt. It is embarrassing and

> **"FOR THE MAN WHO HAS EVERYTHING, THERE IS NOW A CALENDAR TO REMIND HIM WHEN THE PAYMENTS ARE DUE."**

frustrating to have bill collectors calling continually in an attempt to collect unpaid bills. This usually leads to anger, and the individuals begin blaming each other for the predicament they are in. When the creditors begin to repossess vehicles, homes, furniture, and other items, it can really get nasty. Such circumstances can have very negative effects on our Christian testimony. This is not how God wants us to live.

Another reason that financial difficulties are destructive to families is the fact that people must often work night and day to earn enough money to pay their bills. Somebody once said, "For the man who has everything, there is now a calendar to remind him when the payments are due." Working tremendous amounts of overtime or more than one job to make your debt payments can have negative effects on your marriage and on your children. You simply will lack the time necessary to forge strong relationships. Sadly, many people allow

THE VAST MAJORITY OF FINANCIAL PROBLEMS COME FROM PEOPLE LIVING BEYOND THEIR MEANS.

their relationship with God to be affected as well. They just do not have time to attend church because they have to work so often.

It is true that some financial problems are not the result of overspending or poor management. The loss of a job due to downsizing or corporate layoffs, poor health, the premature death of a spouse, unexpected expenses, and other factors may cause people financial hardship. Having said that, the vast majority of financial problems come from people living beyond their means or spending unwisely. This has never been God's plan.

Since this guide is written for young adults, young couples, and others who need to understand the basics of credit management, let this section serve to warn you about the effects of being too far in debt. Again, there is nothing wrong with having nice things; but you must ask yourself what price you are willing to pay. Living according to God's plan and using credit wisely greatly reduces the risk that you will run into trouble later on. God wants us to be free, not in bondage to our creditors. He expects us to be good stewards over the things He has allowed us to have.

YOUR CREDIT RATING

Before you apply for credit, you should have a general understanding of how the approval process works. Volumes have been written about this subject, but my goal is simply to provide you with a broad overview of what a credit rating consists of and some of the things that are taken into consideration.

Many factors are considered when a lender decides whether or not to lend you money or issue you a line of credit. These factors include (but are not limited to) your income, your existing obligations, your residence and occupation stability, and your credit bureau report. All of the factors are combined and they produce a "score" of some sort. In a general sense, the higher your score is, the more likely you are to qualify for a loan. All lenders have their own system, and there are independent companies that provide credit scoring as well. One such company is Fair, Isaac and Company. The score they produce is called the FICO score.

Dawn Sipes, a Vice President with Tucker Mortgage, LLC, prepared the information on the following page that summarizes credit scoring as determined by Fair, Isaac and Company.

CREDIT SCORING
Dawn A. Sipes, Vice President
Tucker Mortgage, LLC

If you've ever wondered what a credit score considers, the following is how your score breaks down as determined by Fair, Isaac and Company.

- 35%–Payment history
- 30%–Amounts owed
- 15%–Length of credit history
- 10%–New credit
- 10%–Types of credit in use

Fair, Isaac's website (*www.fairisaac.com*) lists the leading factors that negatively affect a credit score:

- ✓ Serious delinquency
- ✓ Public record or collection filed *or* Derogatory public record
- ✓ Time since delinquency too recent or unknown
- ✓ Level of delinquency
- ✓ Amount owed on accounts
- ✓ Proportion of balances to credit limits too high
- ✓ Length of time accounts have been established
- ✓ Too many accounts with balances

The more recent the delinquencies, the bigger the impact on the score.

Some items, such as late pays, charge-offs, and collections, may be negotiated directly with the creditor to improve a score. *(continued on following page)*

Certain items cannot be deleted until the time set forth in the Fair Credit Reporting Act. These cannot be removed unless a mistake can be verified and filed with the court.

Bankruptcies–Chapter 7 remains for 10 years. Chapter 13 generally removed after 7 years.
Judgments–Remain on credit for 7 years whether satisfied or not.
Tax liens–Paid *or* released tax liens remain for 7 years.

Another option is to be proactive. Several months or up to one year prior to applying for a loan:

- ✓ Avoid opening new accounts or applying for credit.
- ✓ Pay down balances on revolving accounts to less than 50% of the limit.
- ✓ Make all financing applications for an item within 14 days of one another.

As you become more knowledgeable about credit scoring and how it works, you will be better equipped to pursue a strategy to improve your score and help you obtain a loan at the best rate possible.

Having a good score will sometimes allow you to qualify for better interest rates and more flexible payment arrangements. Qualifying for better interest rates can amount to big savings! Over the life of a $100,000 thirty-year mortgage, just one-half of a percent will save you more than $12,000 in interest.

Your credit report is tracked by a credit bureau, which gathers and monitors information regarding your payment history and habits from companies that you do business with. Your credit report will reflect how timely you are in making your payments, how much credit you have available, how much of your available credit you are using, any unpaid or

> **YOUR CREDIT REPORT IS LIKE A SHADOW; IT WILL FOLLOW YOU AROUND THROUGHOUT YOUR LIFE.**

overdue accounts, past bankruptcy filings, judgments against you, tax liens, and other information. The credit bureau compiles a report on you through information gathered from banks, financial institutions, stores, and other means. This report is checked each time you apply for credit. It is also often checked when you are applying for a new job or for admission to a college or university.

Your credit report is like a shadow; it will follow you around throughout your life. It can significantly affect your ability to borrow money or qualify for lower interest rates, and it may even affect your ability to qualify for some jobs. Because of this, it is very important to keep your credit report clean.

Many people do not realize it, but **every time you apply for a credit card or a loan it has an impact on your credit score.** Keep this in mind the next time a department store clerk offers you a 10% discount off of your purchase if you will apply for the store's credit card. It may cost you much more than the 10% you will save on that relatively small purchase when you apply for a vehicle or a home loan later. Also, do not apply for every "pre-approved" credit card offer you receive in your mailbox. Make sure you close or cancel any accounts that are no longer being used. (Get a written statement from the lender that the account is closed with a zero balance.)

Credit was once difficult to obtain, but now you may receive several credit card offers in your mail each week. Even high school and college students receive offers to apply for credit cards. Since young adults have often not learned to discipline themselves, easy access to credit can be a very dangerous thing in many ways. It is very easy for them to abuse their credit cards and find themselves in financial trouble very early in life. However, young adults are not the only ones who fall victim to having too many credit cards. Credit cards have been the ruin of many mature adults as well.

Any debts that are outstanding will show up until they are paid in full. If you develop delinquent accounts, they will stay on your credit report for seven years, even after they have been paid off. Missed payments are reflected in your credit rating, so make sure you pay on time. Ignoring the statements and phone calls will not make the bills go away. Your creditors will do whatever they can to force you to repay your outstanding accounts. You spent it and you are responsible for it. Remember, *"The wicked borroweth, and payeth not again." (Psalms 37:21)* Make sure you fulfill your obligations.

The best way to avoid getting yourself into trouble is to control your spending. Do not spend money that you do not have. Resist the urge to buy things on impulse, and *never* buy something just so that you can keep up with someone else.   If you do borrow money or use credit cards, be sure that you make your payments on time.   Wise credit management requires discipline, moderation, and self-control.   The Bible instructs us to exercise all of these things. *(Phi. 4:5, 1 Cor. 7:31, Gal. 5:24, Lu. 21:34, 2 Pet. 1:5-7)*

There are three major credit rating companies in the United States.   They are Trans Union, Experian, and Equifax.   By law, you have a right to see your credit report.   It is wise to check your credit report before applying for a loan to make a major purchase such as a home or vehicle.   This allows you to discover and correct any mistakes that may appear on your report.   Many experts recommend reviewing your credit report at least once a year.   Here is the contact information for the three largest credit bureaus:

Equifax
Credit Information Services
PO Box 740241
Atlanta, GA 30374
1-800-685-1111
www.equifax.com

Experian
National Consumer Assistance Center
PO Box 2104
Allen, TX 75013
1-888-397-3742
www.experian.com

Trans Union LLC
Consumer Disclosure Center
PO Box 1000
Chester, PA 19022
1-800-888-4213
www.transunion.com

DISCUSSION/REVIEW QUESTIONS

1.   Discuss the Biblical principles that were violated in Case Study I.

2.   How should Mary correct her problem?

3.   Discuss how a negative credit report can affect you.

4.   What does the Bible say about repaying debts that you owe?

5.   How long will delinquent accounts remain on your credit report?

6.   Do delinquent accounts remain on your report even after they are repaid?

7.   What causes the vast majority of financial problems?

8.   Does a credit card you applied for and received affect your credit report even if you have never used it?

9.   What do statistics reveal about the impact of financial problems on marital success?

10.   *"Neither a borrower nor a lender be"* comes from what book of the Bible?

11.   List some of the ways that credit can be a benefit to you.

12.   Discuss how credit problems can affect your Christian witness.

Note to Discussion Leader: *Questions 1, 2,3, 11 and 12 should be helpful discussion questions.*

Credit Cards

*I*n many ways we are dependent upon credit cards. It is difficult to book flights, make hotel reservations, rent cars, order items from catalogs, or shop via the internet without them. Almost every place you eat, shop, lodge, or go for recreation will accept a credit card. They are convenient and helpful

CREDIT CARDS PRESENT GREAT RISK TO YOUR FINANCIAL WELL-BEING.

in many ways. Despite all of the conveniences they offer, credit cards also present great risk to your financial well-being if they are not used wisely and responsibly.

In this chapter we will discuss some of the advantages and disadvantages of credit cards. We will examine how credit cards work and what charges and fees you will pay. We will also take a closer look at some of the dirty tricks that credit card companies play on their customers. Finally, we will give you some pointers on what you should look for when you are choosing a credit card.

CASE STUDY II

Jim and Brenda have been happily married for five years, and both of them have full-time jobs that pay well. They have two children. Jim is an avid golfer, and Brenda enjoys gardening. They have always lived comfortably and stayed within their budget. Although they are renting now, they hope to buy a home soon.

Recently, Jim replied to an offer he received in the mail for a credit card. The card offered an introductory rate of 1.9% interest on all purchases and balance transfers for the first twelve months. They had no outstanding balances, but Jim had been considering buying a new set of golf clubs. He thought this might be a good way to buy them without using money he had stuck back for a rainy day. After all, the interest rate was only 1.9%; and he could pay it off before the twelve-month period was over. Jim had also been thinking about buying some new accessories for his pickup truck.

Because of Jim and Brenda's good credit history, the credit card company issued a card with a credit limit of $10,000. The paperwork that came with the card explained all the details of the account. It told how the interest rates are calculated (after the introductory period) and how various fees and charges are determined. It also stated that the second time a payment was received late, the interest rate would be increased to 24.9%. Because Jim planned to pay the balance off, he did not read the "Terms and Conditions" very carefully.

Jim purchased his golf clubs and also bought a few items for his truck. Within six months they had accumulated over $7,500 on the card by purchasing new furniture, clothes, and other items they had not budgeted for. The interest rate was just too low to pass up.

Brenda has been sick and hasn't worked for a month. Most of the money that they intended to repay the balance with has been used, and they still have a balance of $5,000. In addition to the $2,500 they paid, they have been paying the minimum monthly payments. Last month, Brenda forgot to mail the payment on time; it was received late. This month, she mailed it on time but forgot about the holiday; the payment was received late again. When she called to complain about the late-fee, the company agreed to reverse the $29.00 fee because of the mix-up. Brenda assumed all was well.

On this statement Jim noticed that the finance charges were over $100, and the interest rate has increased to 24.9%. When he called to inquire, he was told about the late payment clause in the agreement. Now Jim is afraid that they will not be able to pay the card balance. He can't afford to golf, and the new home is out of the question. Jim is very angry with Brenda for this; he feels that it is entirely her fault.

First, let's discuss some of the advantages of having a credit card. We have already mentioned some of them, but here are a few more:

- They eliminate the need to carry large amounts of cash.
- They are accepted almost everywhere.
- They are great to use in emergencies.
- They provide an excellent way to keep track of where you are spending your money.
- They can give you "freebies," such as frequent flier miles, discounts for rental cars and hotels, gift certificates, and other benefits.
- They often provide extended warranties or theft replacement coverage on items purchased with them.

What could possibly be wrong with something that provides so many benefits? The answer to that is, "Nothing! As long as you use it responsibly." For all of the benefits that credit cards provide, they also have many dangers.

Some dangers of credit cards include:

- You end up spending money that you do not have.
- They make it much easier to yield to "Instant Gratification."
- They increase "Impulse Buying."
- They make it easier to confuse "wants" and "needs."

Next, it is important to understand how credit cards work. In the simplest terms, the issuer of the credit card is extending a loan to the person who holds the card. The issuer will usually establish a certain spending limit when they issue the card to you. You can use the card anytime you want to and are allowed to borrow up to the preset spending limit.

Most cards offer a certain "grace period" during which you can pay off the entire balance after you receive your monthly statement. (See the glossary for details on the grace period.) Grace periods vary depending on the card, but as a general rule they are thirty days. If you pay off the entire balance by the due date, then you do not have to pay any interest or finance charges. If you do not pay the entire balance, then interest charges will be added on top of the balance that you already owe. These interest charges also vary depending on the card but may be as high as 25%. Some cards charge an annual fee, which is assessed whether you use the card or not.

In a moment, we will discuss some of the things you should be aware of regarding the use of credit cards. We will also examine the things you should look at when deciding which card to apply for (if you decide to carry a card).

But first, let's examine some principles related to the use of credit cards. As I have already mentioned, they can present great risk to your financial well-being if they are not used correctly. Well-known financial counselor and author, Larry Burkett, suggests that a person or couple who is going to use credit cards should make three simple vows:

1.   Never use your credit cards to buy anything that is not in your budget for the month. So first, you should have a budget.

2.   Pay your credit cards off every month with no exception.

3.   The first month you're unable to pay the credit cards, destroy them.

If you take these vows, You will never have a problem with credit cards.[3]

These rules are the ideal, and following them will put you in the ideal position—a position of control. As we have discussed before, being a good steward requires discipline and self-control. If you will use good judgment and be responsible with your credit cards, then you will be able to take advantage of the conveniences they provide.

If you do not pay the outstanding balance in full each month, then you will begin paying interest on that balance. Since the minimum payments are usually only 2-3% of the outstanding balance, paying it off may be very difficult if you only make the minimum monthly payment. The interest just keeps accumulating, and you are paying *interest* on the *interest* that is accumulating in addition to the interest on the money you actually spent. Additionally, you will begin to incur "over-limit fees" if you do not pay enough each month to keep your outstanding balance below your credit limit. Notice the example on the following page.

---

[3]Larry Burkett, *Answers to Your Family's Financial Questions* (Pomona, CA: 1987) 77

JOHN'S MASTERCARD ACCOUNT

Credit Limit: $2,000

Charges this month: $1,975

Available Credit: $25.00

Minimum payment due (2%): $39.50

Grace Period: 30 days

Interest Rate: 18.9%

Late Payment Fee: $29.00

Over-Limit Fee: $29.00

Let's look at a couple of scenarios using the preceding information. First, let's assume that John pays the entire balance within the thirty-day grace period. If John does this (recommended), he will incur no finance charges; his available credit will again be $2,000.

However, let's assume that John does not have the money to pay the entire amount and decides to only pay the minimum amount due, $39.50, which is 2% of the outstanding balance. ($1,975 - $39.50 = $1,935.50) At the end of the thirty-day grace period, the credit card issuer is going to add finance charges at an annual rate of 18.9% on the remaining outstanding balance. The way that this rate is calculated will vary from card to card, but for this example we will assume that the card uses an average daily balance calculation. To figure this, they will divide the annual interest rate by the number of days in the year to determine the daily periodic interest rate. (18.9% / 365= .0517%) Then they multiply the periodic interest rate by the average daily balance (which we will assume to be $1,975). In this example we have .0517% x $1,975= $1.021. The result of this calculation is then multiplied by the number of days in the billing cycle (usually thirty) to determine the finance charges that will be added to your account. In this case we have $1.021 x 30 = $30.63 of finance charges. This amount would be added to his remaining balance of $1,935.50, and his new balance would be $1,966.13. His finance charges for the next month would be calculated on the average daily balance for that billing cycle, and so on.

Obviously, if John charges anything else and does not send in more than the minimum monthly payment, then he will be in danger of incurring an additional fee for being over his credit limit. He is also paying 18.9% interest on the outstanding balance. If he happens to be late, he will be charged an additional $29.00 late fee. Also, some cards will increase the interest rate if you are late. If that happens, then your rate may be 25% or higher!

Sound complicated?   It is!   And that is one of the disadvantages of credit card bills that are not paid in full each month. Many people have ended up in extreme financial difficulty because they did not understand how their credit cards worked. It is like the proverbial snowball rolling down the hill. Once you get started down the slippery slope, it can be very difficult to stop before you crash at the bottom.

While Mr. Burkett's admonition to destroy the credit cards the first time you fail to pay the balance in full may seem harsh, it is the *ideal* way to ensure that you do not get into trouble. Unless you are using the cards for things that are not included in your budget, his recommendation should be possible because you have already allocated funds to pay the bill.

Approximately one trillion dollars is owed to credit card issuers in the United States at an average interest rate of 18%. Nearly 70 percent of card holders carry large balances on their cards.

> **APPROXIMATELY ONE TRILLION DOLLARS IS OWED TO CREDIT CARD ISSUERS IN THE UNITED STATES AT AN AVERAGE INTEREST RATE OF 18%.**

The interest on these balances profits the card issuers nearly 200 million dollars each day. Experts say that once a person becomes eight hundred or more dollars in debt on a credit card, the issuer has them for life. Since most of us live at the level of our income, even eight hundred dollars can be difficult to pay off. In reality though, the average American owes more than two thousand dollars at a rate of 18%.[4] Does that sound like financial freedom to you?

"The rich ruleth over the poor, and the borrower is servant to the lender." (Proverbs 22:7)

---

[4]John F. MacArthur, Jr., *Whose Money Is It Anyway? A Biblical Guide to Using God's Wealth* (Nashville: Word, 2000) 47

CREDIT CARD FACTS

We have already mentioned several things that can affect your credit card balance. The following list will make you familiar with several "tricks of the trade" that you need to keep in mind. For the most part, paying off your balance each month will eliminate fees and interest; but there are exceptions to that rule of thumb. While some of these things may seem unfair, they are legal. The only choice you have is to stay informed.

- Credit card issuers will often solicit you to apply for a particular card with many fantastic benefits. However, they will issue you a card that has different terms. If a card is not what you want, do not use it or activate it. Call the company and cancel it immediately.

- Credit card companies often change their payment mailing address. By the time your payment is forwarded to the new address, you may have passed your due date. This means that you will incur a late charge and/or an increase in your interest rate. Make sure that you use the envelope included with your statement, and always pay early to allow for delays.

- Your card agreement may also require that your payment be received by a certain time on the due date in order to be credited that same day. Again, always pay early to avoid the possibility of your payment arriving late.

- Even rates on "fixed-rate" cards are not really fixed. This only means that they have to give you a fifteen-day notice before they raise the rate. Make sure you read the notices that come with your monthly statement.

- Credit card issuers are always offering you "free gifts." These offers usually come with your monthly statement. Remember that nothing is free! Throw the offers away. They are gimmicks designed to get more of your hard-earned money.

- Credit card issuers will charge you a fee if you exceed your stated credit limit. Be careful when transferring balances to a new card. It is possible for the issuer to make your credit limit the amount of balance you are transferring from an existing card. If they do this, your card will be "maxed out" when you get it. If you use it, you will exceed your limit and you will pay a fee. Be aware of what your limit is before you use the card. As we discussed earlier, paying only the minimum monthly payment can cause this to

> **CASH ADVANCE FEES ARE OUTRAGEOUS!**

  happen also. Pay the balance in full if possible.

- Cash advance fees are outrageous! Do not use your credit card for cash. These transactions usually begin to incur interest charges immediately (there is no grace period), and the rate is generally higher than the rate for purchases. Not only that, you usually have to pay a fee, which is a percentage of the amount of cash you advance. This fee varies but is usually from 2-4%. Additionally, your payments are applied to the purchase balance before they are applied to the cash advance balance, which has a higher rate.

- If you incur a late fee and complain about it, the credit card company will often reverse the late charge for you. Wonderful, right? Not if they raise your interest rate! (Remember Jim and Brenda?) Most credit card agreements give the issuer the right to raise the rate if your payment is late a certain number of times or multiple times within a certain period. On some cards your rate will increase if you are late just once. Pay your bill early to avoid this.

- Credit card companies can raise the rate on your credit card account because of delinquencies in other accounts you may have, such as a car loan. They *can* and *will* check your credit report frequently to see if there is anything negative that will allow them to raise your rate. Keep your other accounts current to avoid this.

- Credit card issuers try to sell you disability coverage, credit card theft insurance, and other insurance type coverages. These are generally not a good idea. You can purchase other coverage elsewhere (if you need it at all) that will be much more effective and much less expensive.

As for theft coverage, as long as you report your card stolen in a timely manner, you are only liable for a maximum of $50.00 with most credit cards.

- Credit card issuers usually set their minimum monthly payment very low. Paying only the minimum can cause you all kinds of problems (refer to pages 31-33) and can keep you making payments on the card forever. Pay your balance off each month to avoid this.

- Many companies lure you in with very low rates, but the rates soon increase. Also, make sure there are no fees for transferring balances to a lower interest rate card. It is generally not a good idea to change cards frequently. Most introductory rates end after six months or a year.

- Some companies charge extra for foreign purchases. If you travel outside the United States, choose a card that does not charge extra for foreign purchases.

- Be aware of your grace period. The grace period is the period of time from the day after your billing cycle ends until your due date. It is *not* a period of time *after* your due date. If you pay your balance in full within this grace period, you will incur no finance charges. Some companies offer grace periods that are less than thirty days. (Please refer to the glossary for a detailed explanation.)

- Do not apply for every "pre-approved" card offer you receive. There is no guarantee that you will be issued the card you applied for. The credit card company may give you a card that is completely different. Also, your credit rating is affected each time you apply for a new card.

CHOOSING A CREDIT CARD

After all of this discussion, you may have decided that you do not even want a credit card. If you can live without it, you will probably be better off. However, if you still think you want to apply for a card, then there are some things you should know before you do. My advice is to search for a card that has the features and benefits you desire. There are literally thousands of cards available. If you have access to the internet, it is a great place to research what is available. You can also take note of advertisements in the mail and in newspapers and magazines. The following is a list of some things to consider when you decide to apply for a credit card:

BEWARE OF LOW INTRODUCTORY RATES!

- Interest rate
  - ▸ Beware of low introductory rates that increase dramatically at the end of the introductory period.
  - ▸ Fixed-rate cards are generally your best option. Although the rate can technically be raised, companies rarely raise the rate on a fixed-rate card. (Unless you violate your credit agreement.)
  - ▸ Variable-rate cards are usually tied in some way to the prime rate. These rates can be extremely high (up to 25%), and you should be aware of the maximum rate (cap) that the issuer can charge. Also, be aware of what causes the rate to increase.

- How is the interest rate calculated?
  - ▸ Most cards use either the average daily balance, the previous balance, or the adjusted balance method of calculation.
  - ▸ Beware of cards that use two-cycle balances. They will charge interest on purchases that were made during the previous billing cycle. You will be paying interest on interest that has already accrued.
- What are the fees?
  - ▸ Annual fee
  - ▸ Late payment fee
  - ▸ Over-limit fee
  - ▸ Transaction fees
  - ▸ Some include inactivity fees.
  - ▸ Some penalize you when you pay off your balance.
- What is the grace period?
  - ▸ The longer the better.
  - ▸ Beware of cards with a very short or nonexistent grace period. (*Important* information regarding the grace period is contained in the glossary.)
- What is the credit limit?
  - ▸ Make sure that the limit is suitable to your financial situation and needs. Remember, do not use it just because it is available.
  - ▸ Cards with extremely low credit limits are dangerous. Remember, you will pay a fee if you exceed your predetermined credit limit.

When you apply for a card, make sure you read all of the "fine print." There are so many cards available, and they all have their own features and benefits. Some will have "reward points" and some even offer a rebate on the purchases that you make. You will have to determine which card is right for you. Be familiar with the *"Terms and Conditions,"* and remember that you do not have to accept a card if it is not what you wanted or applied for. Just make sure that you have the issuer cancel the card if you do not want it.

Keep in mind that the terms and conditions of your card can change. Do not make the mistake of assuming that the way it is issued is how it will remain

> **DON'T MAKE THE MISTAKE OF APPLYING FOR EVERY CARD THAT IS OFFERED TO YOU.**

forever. As previously mentioned, be sure to read the account information notices that come with your monthly statement.

Do not make the mistake of applying for every card that is offered to you. This negatively affects your credit rating, and it can get you in a lot of trouble financially. Personally, I usually only carry one credit card. I have found that it is much simpler and easier to keep track of that way. I only have to pay one bill each month, and there is less danger of me overlooking a change in the terms and conditions of my card. However, do not be married to a particular card. If the issuer is employing some of the tactics we discussed earlier, then you may be better off finding another card. Keeping your account in good standing puts you in a position of control. If you decide to change companies, make sure you cancel the card you are replacing; all open accounts are considered in your credit score.

When you cancel a card or an account, get a written statement from the lender that the account is closed with a zero balance.

Do not hesitate to ask the credit card company to reduce your rate. Often, they will offer you better terms if you inform them that you may change companies. Do not be afraid to change companies if the need arises. Just be sure that you have a legitimate reason because it is generally not a good idea to change cards frequently.

The cards we have discussed so far are referred to as general-use or multipurpose credit cards. Another type of card that is available is a single-purpose card, such as a department store or gasoline card. These cards are issued to be used at a specific store, a group of stores or gas stations, etc. They are similar in many ways to the cards we have already discussed, but they generally **REMEMBER, EVERY CARD YOU HAVE WILL AFFECT YOUR CREDIT RATING.** have much lower credit limits. These cards often have much higher interest rates than general-purpose cards. Many people feel that one general-purpose card is sufficient. Remember, every card you have will affect your credit rating. The more credit cards you have, the greater the risk of misuse and abuse.

In summary, most credit card problems can be avoided by following Larry Burkett's three simple rules. If you will discipline yourself and abide by Biblical principles, then you will avoid the common mistakes that many people make with credit cards. Refuse to become a victim of credit card abuse; control your spending.

DISCUSSION/REVIEW QUESTIONS

1. *a.)* Discuss the mistakes that were made by Jim and Brenda and the effects they may have in Case Study II.

   b.) How can Jim and Brenda solve their problem?

2. Do credit cards pose a great risk to your financial well-being? If so, why?

3. What are some of the advantages of credit cards?

4. What are some of the dangers of credit cards?

5. List five ways in which credit card companies attempt to take advantage of their customers.

6. List Larry Burkett's three rules for credit card use.

7. List five examples of credit card fees.

8. What is the "grace period" on a credit card?

9. Can a credit card company raise the interest rate on your credit card because of delinquencies on other accounts?

10. Explain the difference between a "fixed-rate" and a "variable-rate" card.

11. Can the "Terms and Conditions" on a credit card change?

12. Can the interest rate on a "fixed-rate" card change?

Note to Discussion Leader: *Questions 1,2,3, and 4 should be helpful discussion questions.*

Installment Loans

If we all had a money tree, then I suppose we would not need to borrow money at all. The reality is that most of us need to borrow money from time to time. In this chapter we will explore the following two types of installment loans:

- "Consumer Credit" Loans
- Auto Loans

Installment loans represent the largest category of consumer loans. Everything from automobiles to vinyl siding and stereos can be financed with an installment loan. They are fairly easy to qualify for, and the fixed monthly payment is a convenient way to repay the lender. They are also very profitable to the lending industry.

Credit comes in many forms, but the principles that apply to its use should not change. Although installment loans are usually used to purchase larger items, we should still make our buying decisions based on our need for the item being considered and our ability to repay the amount we borrow. Apply the Biblical principles we have already discussed to installment loans as well.

CASE STUDY III

Bob and Sue are a successful young couple with two children. They both work and they have above average incomes. A year ago, they purchased the new home they had been dreaming about. They have always had good credit and easily qualified for the mortgage. They were very happy in the new home but decided to visit the furniture store downtown to "just look." Their old furniture was still in good shape, but it just didn't seem to fit the look of the new house. They needed something a bit more modern and a little nicer, similar to what their neighbors had. They agreed to just look and not buy.

At the store they fell in love with several items. Although they just came to look, they decided to purchase the items because the store was offering a "Twelve Months Same-As-Cash" financing option. Since they used up the majority of their savings for the down payment on their new house, this financing offer seemed to be just perfect. They figured that they would be able to come up with the money to pay off the loan within twelve months.

The salesperson explained to them that at the end of the twelve months, the interest would be added to the loan retroactive to the purchase date. However, that would only happen if they did not pay off the entire amount before the end of the free period. He said the interest would be 18.9% if they did not pay it off. The interest rate concerned Bob; but since he was confident that they could pay off the loan, they went ahead with their purchase. The financed amount was $6,400.

During the summer Bob realized that their new lawn was much bigger than their old one. Since he was working more overtime to make the new house payment, he did not have nearly as much time as before to mow the lawn with a push mower. The local hardware store was offering a special "Six-Months Same-as-Cash" offer on all new riding lawn mowers one Saturday, so Bob decided to purchase one. As usual, Bob was approved with flying colors because of his good credit. He planned to use his annual bonus to pay off the loan.

Bob just found out that his bonus will be much less than what he expected. He cannot pay off either of his loans before the end of the free period. Their utility bills have increased in the new house, they have a new car, and they just found out they're going to have another baby. Bob and Sue can't see how they are going to make the monthly payments on the loans. They have cancelled their "Faith Promise" missions pledge because they can't afford to pay everything. They're afraid that the furniture and lawn mower will have to be repossessed. It will be embarrassing and it will ruin their good credit. Now they wish they would have waited a few days before deciding to buy. They know that their old furniture and mower were really good enough.

"CONSUMER CREDIT" LOANS

After credit cards, one of the most dangerous forms of debt is what I refer to as the "consumer credit" loan.   By this I am primarily referring to loans or revolving credit accounts arranged through finance companies such as Wells Fargo, Norwest, and others.   These companies usually underwrite the financing that furniture stores, appliance stores, electronics stores, and home improvement stores make available to their customers.

How many times have you noticed a sign that said, "Six Months Same-As-Cash" or "No Payment Till December of 2002" or "No Interest Until Next Year"? These signs are everywhere. They   are   especially

> ## THE THREE-DAY RULE:
>
> **GO HOME AND THINK ABOUT IT FOR THREE DAYS BEFORE YOU MAKE A DECISION TO BUY IT.**

common at stores and places of business that sell higher priced merchandise. Examples include furniture stores, carpet stores, and electronics superstores. Recently, even Wal-mart has begun to offer customers this option on big-ticket items.

There are a number of reasons why these financing offers can cause you problems. Like credit cards, such offers will often entice you to spend money that you do not have. Please don't misunderstand, there are times when these types of purchases are warranted and acceptable.   However, if you are going to take advantage of consumer financing, it should be used to purchase items for which you have budgeted. Consumer financing *should not* be used to purchase items on impulse. Always remember the "Three-day Rule": Go home and think about it for three days before you make a decision to buy something. You will be surprised how many times you decide you do not need it as badly as you had thought. (Remember Bob and Sue?)

The "Same-as-Cash" trend is very dangerous indeed. There are times when it can be used to your advantage, but only if you already have the money set aside to pay off the entire amount of the purchase. In those cases, you can leave your money sitting in an interest-bearing account until it is time to pay off the financed amount. By doing this you continue to earn interest on your money during the period of "free" financing. This is very dangerous.

There are many reasons I say this is dangerous. First, it takes tremendous discipline not to spend the money that is sitting in your account. There are too many "emergencies" which arise, and the money ends up being spent on something else. When that happens, you would have been better off to have paid for the item at the time of purchase because you would not have incurred any interest fees.

Another disadvantage is that if you do not pay off the *entire* balance by the end of the "Same-as-Cash" period, the interest charges you would have normally incurred will be added to your current outstanding balance. The rate is usually 18 to 24%. You will then be paying interest on accumulated interest (this is known as compound interest). These loans can be very difficult to pay off. Additionally, when you factor in the interest charges, you end up paying a very high price for the furniture, carpet, appliance, or other item you purchased. You are usually better off to save the money and pay for the item at the time of purchase. (See the glossary for a detailed explanation.)

If you have exceptional credit, you might be able to obtain an unsecured note from your bank or credit union. Unsecured loans will generally have lower interest rates than finance companies offer; and they are usually figured using a "simple interest" calculation, which keeps you from paying interest on accumulated interest. Such loans are worth considering as an alternative to consumer credit financing.

> **BEWARE OF THE "SAME-AS-CASH" TRAP!**

In addition to the things we have already discussed, another factor comes into play in "Same-as-Cash" scenarios. By the time the loan comes due, the newness and the excitement over your purchase has long since disappeared. In many cases the item may already be damaged or set aside. In extreme cases the item may have already been discarded by the time you have to "pay the fiddler." Very rarely are people as excited to pay off the balance or begin making the monthly payments as they were to make the purchase initially. Consequently, "Same-as-Cash" (deferred interest) loans have a high rate of default. Unless you have specifically budgeted and planned for this type of purchase, do not fall into the "Same-as-Cash" trap.

Once you've financed one item, you may be enticed to finance several more, and the payments may all come due at the same time. If you have purchased several items using consumer financing, you may find yourself with several relatively small monthly payments. Added together, these can really get you off track. Not only that, when you calculate how much money you are spending on interest charges, you may be sorry you chose to finance items you could have lived without.

As with any other form of credit, you should consider the Biblical principles that we have discussed. Keep your budget in mind, and only purchase items for which you have budgeted. Resist the urge to purchase things on impulse, and remember the Three-day Rule. Don't be tricked into an installment loan because of savings from a big sale. Use common sense and pray for God's guidance when you find yourself tempted to purchase something you might be able to live without.

AUTOMOBILE LOANS

Auto loans are among the most common installment loans, and they are usually relatively easy to qualify for. These are referred to as secured loans because the bank holds the title of the vehicle you are buying as security or collateral until the loan is fully repaid. If you fail to make your payments as agreed, the bank or financing company has the right to repossess your vehicle.

The period of time over which you may repay an automobile loan will vary depending on the age of the car. On most new cars you can stretch the payments out over a five-year period (60 months) if you wish. In addition to the 60-month loan, you can choose periods of 48, 36, or 24 months. You may be limited to shorter loan periods on older model pre-owned vehicles.

These loans are usually based on simple interest; and the interest rates will vary based on your credit history, the age of the vehicle, and the prime rate at the time of your purchase. There is usually no penalty for repaying the loan prior to the end of your loan period, but you need to make sure of this when you finance the vehicle. These loans may be underwritten by the automobile manufacturer, your local bank, a bank or finance company that the dealer has a relationship with, or other sources.

> **MAINTAINING A GOOD CREDIT RATING WILL ALLOW YOU TO QUALIFY FOR LOANS WITH THE BEST INTEREST RATES.**

Maintaining a good credit rating will allow you to qualify for loans with the best interest rates. It will also give you additional flexibility with the terms of your loan. A good credit rating will put you in the driver's seat (no pun intended) when it comes time to finance your new vehicle.

Once you have prayerfully considered which vehicle you should buy, you will need to make some decisions about financing that vehicle. Obviously, you should not be buying a vehicle that will stretch you to the limit financially each month. Make sure that you are employing the previously discussed principles related to credit and borrowing money. The following are some things you should keep in mind when you are purchasing a new vehicle:

- The shorter the length (term) of the loan, the less interest you will pay over the life of the loan.
- The shorter the term of the loan, the higher the monthly payment will be.
- Shorter term loans will often provide better interest rates.
- Using the longest possible loan term means you will pay the maximum amount of interest.
- The more money you have for a down payment, the lower your monthly payments will be.
- Financing a vehicle for the longest possible period of time increases the odds that your vehicle will eventually be worth less than you owe on it. When this happens, you are considered "upside down." To avoid this, finance for a shorter length of time; and/or pay a substantial down payment at the time of purchase.
- It is usually not a good idea to purchase extended warranties. They are expensive, they will increase your monthly payments, and they are seldom ever used.
- It is *almost never* a good idea to purchase credit life and disability insurance. This will increase your monthly payment, and you can purchase an individual term insurance policy with a higher death benefit for less than you will pay for credit life insurance (which will only cover the outstanding balance on your auto loan).
- If you have a choice between a rebate and a lower interest rate, you must decide which option will save you the most money. This will depend on what interest rate you qualify for, the length of the loan term, and other factors. You can

calculate monthly payment amounts and total interest by using financial loan calculators on the internet. There are many useful tools at *www.quicken.com/banking_and_credit.*

- Be careful about rolling the unpaid loan balance on your old vehicle into the financing on the new vehicle. Many times this will cause you to be "upside down" when you drive the vehicle off of the dealer's lot. ("Upside down" refers to owing more on a vehicle than it is worth.)
- Resist the urge to "over buy." Purchase a vehicle that you can easily afford without having to worry each month.
- Don't forget to consider the increase in your auto insurance premium. This may affect which car you buy.

Let's look at four variations of a typical auto loan. This will give you an idea of the interest you will pay in different scenarios.

Scenario 1
New Vehicle Purchase Price: $20,000
Interest Rate: 6.9%
Down Payment: $0.00
Loan Period: 60 months
Monthly Payment: $395.08
Total Payments Over Life of Loan: $23,704.80
Total Interest Paid: $3,704.80

Scenario 2
New Vehicle Purchase Price: $20,000
Interest Rate: 6.9%
Down Payment: $0.00
Loan Period: 48 months
Monthly Payment: $478.00
Total Payments Over Life of Loan: $22,944.00
Total Interest Paid: $2,944.00

Scenario 3
New Vehicle Purchase Price: $20,000
Interest Rate: 6.9%
Down Payment: $1,500
Loan Period: 60 months
Monthly Payment: $365.45
Total Payments Over Life of Loan: $21,927.00
Total Interest Paid: $3,427

Scenario 4
New Vehicle Purchase Price: $20,000
Interest Rate: 8.9%
Down Payment: $0.00
Loan Period: 60 months
Monthly Payment: $414.20
Total Payments Over Life of Loan: $24,852.00
Total Interest Paid: $4,852.00

> **ONE OF THE BIGGEST MISTAKES PEOPLE MAKE WHEN MAKING MAJOR PURCHASES IS BUYING BASED ON MONTHLY PAYMENT INSTEAD OF TOTAL PURCHASE PRICE.**

As you can see, the amount of interest you pay changes depending on the length of time, the interest rate, and the amount of money you pay down. You will have to determine what you can afford based on your budget. If you can be content to purchase a lower priced vehicle and finance it for a shorter period of time, you will save money in interest charges. A quality pre-owned vehicle may be your best option.

One of the biggest mistakes people make when making major purchases is buying based on monthly payment instead of total purchase price. When you do this, you usually fail to consider the amount of interest that you are paying on your purchase. I recommend that you multiply the monthly payment amount by the number of months you will have to pay. Compare the amount of your total payments with the purchase price of the vehicle (or other item). The difference will be the amount of interest you will pay over the life of the loan. Then ask yourself if it is worth it. I have talked myself out of making major purchases many times by employing this simple rule. It helps you to avoid the "impulse buy." I can assure you that salespeople will not suggest it. They know that it is easier to sell their product if they can get you to focus on the monthly payment. Remember, **lengthening the loan period lowers the *payment*; but it does not lower the *cost*.** It actually increases the cost by adding more interest. Keep this in mind, and it will save you money throughout your life. Also, remember that a vehicle is a depreciating asset. This means that the longer you owe for it, the more money you will be wasting.

If you are disciplined enough to pay off an auto loan before you buy another vehicle, it is a great idea to contribute the money you had been paying for monthly payments to a "car fund" instead of going on a spending spree. If you do this, you will accumulate money toward your next vehicle purchase. This will allow you to make a larger down payment or even pay cash the next time, thereby saving you money on interest charges.

Rev. Tom O'Daniel, Executive Vice President of Indiana Bible College, is often asked for advice by students considering the purchase of a new vehicle. He asks them to estimate the amount of additional monthly payment they will pay for a newer one. He then advises them to place that money in a special account for six months while they continue to drive their existing vehicle. The money that accumulates can be used for the down payment on the new one, thereby lowering their monthly payment and interest charges. *Ideally*, the student will continue to drive their existing vehicle beyond the initial six-month period, continuing to save until they can afford to pay cash for the new one. In any case, they are better off because they have cash to apply toward their purchase.

I mentioned this earlier in the list of things to consider, but I want to bring it up again as we close this section: Always consider the fact that your automobile insurance will usually increase when you buy a new vehicle. This has to be taken into consideration when you determine what kind of vehicle to buy. Insurance premiums are not based entirely on the cost of a vehicle; cost is only one of the factors considered. The type of vehicle, horsepower, theft rating, and many other factors also play a role. In other words, two vehicles might cost the same; but the insurance premium might by considerably higher on one compared with the other. Always call your insurance agent and get an estimate *before* you commit to purchasing a new vehicle. You must be able to afford *both* the payment on the vehicle each month *and* the insurance premiums.

One last note, you will have to pay sales tax and licensing fees in most states. Keep this in mind, and be sure you can afford it. Resist the urge to buy a new vehicle on impulse. Don't be influenced to make a major purchase just because someone is having a "sale." Carefully consider the things we have discussed in this section before making a decision to buy a new vehicle.

Discussion/Review Questions

1. What is an installment loan?

2. Explain the "Same-as-Cash" concept.

3. Discuss the mistakes that were made by Bob and Sue in Case Study III.

4. What rule could have helped Bob and Sue to avoid their predicament?

5. How can Bob and Sue recover from their mistakes?

6. Explain the relationship between the length of the loan and the monthly payment on an installment loan.

7. Does lowering the monthly payment lower the cost? Why or why not?

8. What is one of the biggest mistakes people make when making a major purchase?

9. Maintaining a good credit rating will allow you to qualify for what?

10. What will cause you to pay the maximum amount of interest on an auto loan?

11. Why is it generally not a good idea to purchase extended warranties?

12. In addition to the monthly payment on your loan, what other expenses should you consider when purchasing a vehicle?

Note to Discussion Leader: *Questions 3,5,6,7 and 8 should be helpful discussion questions.*

Home Mortgages

SHOULD I RENT OR BUY?

Generally speaking, purchasing a home is better than renting a place to live. You are creating equity in an asset that will generally appreciate in value, and often you can sell it for a profit later on. Also, the equity that you develop over time can be used as a financing tool.

Having said that, there are times when buying a home is not a practical choice and renting is the best option. There are closing costs, fees, and realtor commissions each time you buy or sell a home. A good rule of thumb is that it takes two years of appreciation to recover your purchase costs. If you will be relocating frequently, it may not be in your best interest to own a home. In addition to the costs you will incur, the home may or may not appreciate in value over the short term. Also, you will pay taxes and maintenance. In cases like this, the cost of owning a home may actually be greater than the cost of renting.

CASE STUDY IV

Steve and Cathy have been married for three years. They are both college graduates and have been very responsible financially. Soon after they were married, Steve and Cathy sat down and identified several goals that they wanted to reach. One of those goals was to pay off their student loans within a year. Another was to buy a house within the first five years of their marriage.

Steve and Cathy realized that it would require some sacrifices on their part if they were to accomplish their objectives. Although Cathy really wanted a new vehicle, she decided that it would be best to wait until after she had paid off her student loans. The car she was driving had over a hundred thousand miles on it, but it did not have any significant mechanical problems. She felt it would last for a while.

Steve considered purchasing a motorcycle when he received a signing bonus at the firm he went to work for. Instead, he decided that it would be better to apply the money to his student loans. He realized that the motorcycle could wait since it was not a priority.

Things went well at work for Steve and Cathy, and they were able to pay off their student loans within ten months of being married. They were very excited about being out from under that burden and considered buying some new furniture to celebrate. They even went to the furniture store to look around. The store was offering some special financing, and they were very tempted to purchase a new living room suite. They opted to think it over and decided after a day or two that they really did not need the furniture after all. They felt that it would be better to save for the down payment on a house.

Last month, Steve and Cathy decided they would start looking for houses and went to seek pre-approval for a mortgage. They were approved for up to $125,000. They have found two or three houses they really like in that price range. They have also found a house they like well enough for about $100,000. Although it is not quite as fancy, it is in a good neighborhood; and they feel that they could resell it easily. Steve's brother and his wife just purchased a house in one of the subdivisions at the upper end of Steve and Cathy's price range. They are encouraging Steve and Cathy to purchase one nearby.

Cathy has done some calculations and has determined that the only way they can afford the monthly payment on the more expensive house is with a 30-year adjustable-rate mortgage. However, if they buy the lower priced house, they can finance it with a 15-year fixed-rate mortgage. She has discovered that this will save them over $100,000 in interest charges, and it will also keep them from worrying about an interest rate increase. Having decided this is the best option, they will soon close on their new house—two years ahead of schedule.

You will need to determine what is best in your situation. For the reasons mentioned earlier or other reasons, you may decide you would be better off to rent. There is certainly nothing wrong with that. If you decide to rent for now but want to purchase a home in the future, then you should begin saving money to apply to your down payment and closing costs. Having a substantial amount of money set aside for this purpose will give you more options when you decide to purchase a home.

I HAVE DECIDED TO BUY. WHAT NOW?

Once you have made a decision to buy a home, you will begin the process of finding the one you want. A detailed analysis of which home you should

PURCHASING A HOME IS A LONG-TERM COMMITMENT, SO CHOOSE WISELY. THE DECISIONS YOU MAKE TODAY WILL STILL BE IMPACTING YOUR FINANCES FOR MANY YEARS TO COME.

buy is beyond the scope of this discussion, but you should keep the Biblical principles we have discussed in mind. You should not purchase a home that is too expensive for your budget. Prayerfully consider your options, and ask the Lord to guide you as you make your decisions. Remember that you will be responsible for the monthly payment. Do not commit to something that you cannot easily afford. Do not feel pressured to keep up with someone else. You can always upgrade as your financial situation improves. If you have to work many hours of overtime or get an additional job to make your monthly payment, then you may not get to enjoy your new home nearly as much as you thought. Purchasing a home is a long-term commitment, so choose wisely. The decisions you make today will still be impacting your finances for many years to come.

When you have decided on the home that you want, you will have to decide how to go about paying for it. Unless you are blessed with the finances to pay cash for your new home, then you will have to apply for a mortgage. There are countless banks and mortgage companies that will be anxious to assist you. Regardless of where you choose to do business, there are two basic choices you must make: 1) The length of your mortgage, 2)Whether you want a fixed or a variable interest rate.

LENGTH OF MORTGAGE TERM

Although there are many variations, the two most common mortgage periods are fifteen and thirty years. As with auto loans, the shorter the mortgage term, the higher the monthly payment; but you will pay significantly less interest over the life of the mortgage. Deciding which term is best for you will depend on several factors. The most important factor will be how much you can afford to pay each month. You can afford a more expensive home if you stretch the payments out over thirty years, but you will pay far more in interest charges by doing so. Again, prayerfully consider what is best for you. Financially, you might be better off to settle for a lesser house and finance for a shorter period of time. (Case Study IV)

Remember the point that we made earlier: ***One of the biggest mistakes people make when making major purchases is buying based on monthly payment instead of total purchase price.***

FIXED-RATE MORTGAGES

With a fixed-rate mortgage, you are locked in at a particular interest rate for the entire term of the mortgage. This removes the risk that the principal and interest portion of your payment will change over time. However, on a fixed-rate mortgage you are usually required to escrow your property taxes and your homeowner's insurance. This means that your mortgage company pays these expenses when they are due from money that you send each month (in addition to the principal and interest on your loan). This additional money is placed in an "escrow account," and it is disbursed as necessary. Taxes and insurance may increase over time. If they do, the escrow portion of your payment will be increased to cover the cost. In any case, because the principal and interest portion of your payment never changes, you are able to plan your budget more precisely.

(Fixed-rate mortgages are often more difficult to qualify for.)

ADJUSTABLE-RATE MORTGAGES

Interest rates on these mortgages (also referred to as ARMs) are subject to change over time. What causes your rate to change will depend on the specific mortgage you have, but ARM rates are usually linked to the prime rate or another financial index. These mortgages will generally offer lower interest rates than fixed-rate mortgages in the beginning, but keep in mind that your rate may increase (or decrease) over time. Adjustable-rate mortgages are often used by people who plan to move within a few years, but they may be appropriate for anyone.

There are many variations of these mortgages. For instance, most lenders will offer a 5/1 ARM. This means that the rate is fixed initially for five years and then it can change each year after that. These loans are usually amortized over a thirty-year period. (Amortization is the gradual and systematic reduction of debt by application of equal periodic payments.)

If you are thinking about using an ARM, you should make sure that you know the maximum rate that you could be charged. This is referred to as the "cap." Knowing the cap is important because a significant increase in interest rates could cause you to be unable to make your monthly mortgage payments.

To illustrate this point, let's assume that you qualify for a $100,000 5/1 ARM at an initial rate guarantee of 6.9%. The monthly payment (principal and interest) would be $658.60. Now let's assume that the rate cap is 11.9% and interest rates increase during the five-year period of your initial rate guarantee. At the end of that guaranteed period, your rate is increased to the maximum amount, 11.9%. Your monthly payment at that interest rate would be $1,020.92, an increase of $362.32 per month. If your budget would not handle the additional costs, then an adjustable-rate mortgage might not be the best option for you in that scenario.

As I said earlier, there are many variations of these mortgages. Some have caps on how much the interest rate can increase in any one year, etc. You will have to determine what works best for you. Always figure the worst-case scenario before you make a decision.

CLOSING COSTS

Regardless of what type or length of mortgage you choose, there will be certain costs and fees associated with finalizing your purchase or "closing" your loan. (Closing refers to the point at which the transfer of property from one owner to another occurs.) You must be careful not to overlook the "closing costs" that you will be responsible for in addition to the purchase price of your new home. Some of the more common fees are:

- Application Fee, a fee the lender charges for processing your loan application.
- Appraisal Fee, the cost of appraising your home to determine its market value. You may request a copy of the appraisal report.
- Attorney Fees, any fees for legal services associated with the transaction.
- Credit Report Fee, the amount the credit bureau who provided your credit report charges the lender.
- Document Preparation Fee, this includes the costs of preparing documents, notary services, etc.
- Homeowner's Insurance, you will usually be required to pay the first annual homeowner's premium at or before closing.
- Inspection Fees, the lender will usually require termite or property inspections to verify the condition of the property and buildings. These inspections protect you by discovering potential defects or conditions that might cost thousands of dollars to remedy or repair later. If serious defects are discovered, you may be able to back out of the purchase.

- Interest, you will be responsible for "odd-day" interest. This is the interest per day between closing and the day your first mortgage payment is due.

- Lock-in Fee, a fee you pay the lender for guaranteeing you a certain interest rate. If you do not "lock-in" your rate when you apply for the mortgage, then you will pay the interest rate that is current at the time of closing.

- Mortgage Origination Fee, this fee is often referred to as "points." One percent of the amount borrowed equals one point. Lenders generally charge up to four points. Sometimes you can pay points to "buy down" or lower your interest rate. You will need to determine what is best for you depending on current rates, other costs, etc.

- Private Mortgage Insurance (PMI), generally, if you do not have at least 20 percent of your purchase price for a down payment, then you will have to pay for PMI. This insurance helps to protect the lender if you default on your mortgage. The first PMI premium is usually due at closing and will vary depending on the amount of down payment you make.

- Property Taxes, the property taxes on your home will be prorated to the date of closing. The seller is responsible for any taxes due prior to closing, and the buyer is responsible for any taxes due after closing.

- Recording Fees, the fees that are charged to legally record a property deed.

- Survey Fee, sometimes a property survey is required.

- Tax Service Fee, this fee covers the cost of researching the property taxes and determining who is responsible for what.

- Title Charges, this will include your title insurance and any attorney fees that may be necessary. The title insurance policy protects you in the event of discrepancies in the title of the property. This is often split between buyer and seller but may be paid entirely by the seller.
- Miscellaneous Fees, may include flood certification (to determine if the property is in a flood zone), faxes, overnight delivery of documents, or other clerical fees.

The total closing costs will vary depending on the purchase amount and several other factors. Your lender will provide you with a "Good Faith Estimate" of what the closing costs will be when you apply for your loan. Although this estimate may not be exact, it is usually fairly close. Some of the charges I have outlined, such as the homeowner's insurance, interest, and property taxes, are actually "pre-paid expenses" instead of costs; but they still have to be paid at closing so I have included them here.

Some of these costs will vary from lender to lender. For example, some lenders will waive the loan application fee and others will waive the points. The mortgage industry is very competitive, and if you are smart you will use this to your advantage. Shop around for the best rates and the best closing costs. Lenders will often meet or beat the rates and costs offered by other lenders. As I mentioned in a previous section, over the life of a $100,000 thirty-year mortgage, just one-half of a percent will save you more than $12,000 in interest. You may also be able to negotiate and get the seller to pay some or all of the closing costs. This is especially true if the property has been on the market for a considerable period of time.

HYPOTHETICAL GOOD FAITH ESTIMATE OF CLOSING COSTS

Lender: ABC Mortgage Company   Loan Amount: $102,000
Property Address: 4212 Apple Lane   Interest Rate: 7.060%
Borrower(s): Jerry and Susan Jones   Type: Conventional
Closing Date: May 3, 2002   5/1 ARM

The costs listed are estimates—the actual costs may be more or less.

Items Payable in Connection With Loan:

Loan Origination Fee	$ 500.00
Discount Points	.00
Appraisal Fee	350.00
Credit Report/Scoring Fee	19.20
Processing Fee	425.00
Tax Service Fee	85.00
Flood Certification	19.50

Items Required by Lender to be Paid at Settlement:

Per diem Interest for: 29 days @ 20.02	580.58
Homeowner's Insurance Premium	480.00
Property Tax (2 months)	236.12
Mortgage Insurance (premium for 1 month)	100.00

Title Charges:

Closing Fee	200.00
Document Preparation	50.00
Attorney Fee	200.00
Title Insurance	125.00

Government Recording and Transfer Charges:

Recording/Filing Fees	42.00

Additional Settlement Charges:

Survey	150.00
Pest Inspection	75.00
Property Inspection	150.00
Overnight Mail Fees	50.00

Total Estimated Funds Needed for Closing:

$3,837.40

We have not exhausted this topic by any means, and there are many resources at your local library or online that can provide you with more detailed information regarding home mortgages. I would recommend that you find a good book on the subject before you make any permanent decisions. It is also a good idea to obtain pre-approval from a bank or mortgage company *before* you start shopping for your new home. If you find out how much money they will lend you, then you can shop for your home accordingly.

Notice the following examples of fifteen and thirty-year mortgages, paying attention to the amount of interest paid on each.

Scenario 1
15-Year Mortgage, $100,000, 6.9%
Monthly Payment: $893.25
Total Payments Over Life of Mortgage: $160,785
Total Interest Paid: $60,785

Scenario 2
30-Year Mortgage, $100,000, 6.9%
Monthly Payment: $658.60
Total Payments Over Life of Mortgage: $237,096
Total Interest Paid: $137,096

Scenario 3
15-Year Mortgage, $75,000, 6.9%
Monthly Payment: $669.94
Total Payments Over Life of Mortgage: $120,589.20
Total Interest Paid: $45,589.20

Scenario 4
30-Year Mortgage, $125,000, 6.9%
Monthly Payment: $823.25
Total Payments Over Life of Mortgage: $296,370
Total Interest Paid: $171,370

As you can see in Scenario 2, the amount of interest you pay over the life of a thirty-year mortgage is significant. By reducing the purchase amount by $25,000 (Scenario 3) and using a fifteen-year mortgage, your payment is within just a few dollars of the amount you would pay for the thirty-year mortgage in Scenario 2. However, look at the difference in total interest paid between Scenario 2 and Scenario 3. You would save $91,506.80 in interest. (Scenario 1 and Scenario 4 contain the figures that correspond with Steve and Cathy's calculations in Case Study IV.)

It is a good idea to look at comparisons like this before you buy. Most personal finance software programs (such as Quicken and Microsoft Money) have loan calculators that will provide the calculations for you. All you have to do is enter the interest rate, loan amount, and period of the loan. Many websites provide calculators as well (*www.quicken.com/banking_and_credit*). If you do not have access to loan calculators, then banks and finance companies will usually provide the information to you over the phone.

DISCUSSION/REVIEW QUESTIONS

1. Why is it so important to choose wisely when purchasing a home?
2. Which of the mortgage terms we discussed will cost you the most in interest charges?
3. When might renting be a better option than buying?
4. Identify and discuss all of the things that Steve and Cathy did well in Case Study IV.
5. Explain the difference between a fixed-rate mortgage and an adjustable-rate mortgage.

Note to Discussion Leader: Questions 3 and 4 should be helpful discussion questions.

Conclusions

*P*reviously, I made the statement that credit can be a great friend or a terrible enemy; it all depends on how you manage it. I sincerely hope that you have discovered a few ways to manage your credit more effectively.

We have certainly not exhausted the topics that we looked at. There has been much research and analysis completed on all of the things that we have touched on here, and many opinions have been offered. Also, there are many additional aspects to managing your credit and your

> **GOOD STEWARDSHIP REQUIRES DISCIPLINE AND SELF-CONTROL.**

personal finances. However, I do hope that you know more now than you did when you picked this guide up.

Above all, make sure that you put God first in all of your planning and decision making. Be diligent to follow the principles outlined in His Word, and He will provide you with wisdom and understanding to make the right decisions. We have mentioned it often on the preceding pages, but it bears repeating here: "Good stewardship requires discipline and self-control." Do not live beyond your means, and you will not become a slave to the material system of this world.

If you borrow money, pay it back; it is your responsibility as a Christian and a righteous person. If you do not, you will be counted among the wicked. *"The wicked borroweth, and payeth not again: but the righteous sheweth mercy, and giveth." (Psalms 37:21)* In my opinion, it is morally wrong not to repay the debts that you owe. Would you want to be repaid if you were the lender? Not only will you

> **MANAGING YOUR CREDIT WISELY WILL GIVE YOU MORE FLEXIBILITY TO PURSUE GOD'S WILL IN YOUR LIFE.**

be counted among the wicked, but you also risk ruining your name. You can destroy your Christian witness by irresponsible financial behavior. **Don't ruin your good name with bad credit.** Proverbs 22:1 says, *"A good name is rather to be chosen than great riches, and loving favor rather than silver and gold."*

Always remember to seek God first. *"But seek ye first the kingdom of God, and His righteousness; and all these things shall be added unto you." (Matthew 6:33)* Managing your credit wisely will give you more flexibility to pursue God's will in your life. Dr. James A. Jones, who has pastored for over thirty years and retired from a professorship at Indiana Central University, recently made the following statement to me, "I wonder if one of the greatest destroyers of ministries is debt? I have observed so many ministries that were destroyed by excessive debt." If you are not trapped under a mountain of debt, you will have more freedom to do the things that God asks of you and will have more latitude in your giving also.

The profound words of Jesus, spoken all those years ago, still ring in our ears today, *"²⁹The first of all the commandments is, Hear, O Israel; The Lord our God is one Lord: ³⁰And thou shalt love the Lord thy God with all thy heart, and with all thy soul, and with all thy mind, and with all thy strength: this is the first commandment. ³¹And the*

DON'T RUIN YOUR GOOD NAME WITH BAD CREDIT.

second is like, namely this, Thou shalt love thy neighbor as thyself. There is none other commandment greater than these." (Mark 12:29-31) If you love God more than anything else, it will be reflected in your finances. If you love your neighbor as yourself, you will be diligent to repay what you owe.

My prayer is that you will apply Biblical principles to the decisions you make in your life. Allow God to lead you; He does not make mistakes! Apply the principles contained in this guide, and you will enjoy the benefits of being in control of your debt. I will never forget a statement that was made by Rev. Danny Leslie, a pastor in Yakima, Washington. He said, "Desire makes a way; lack of desire makes an excuse." This is certainly the case with good stewardship. May God bless you as you journey down the road on your way to becoming a good steward.

"³⁶For what shall it profit a man, if he shall gain the whole world, and lose his own soul? ³⁷Or what shall a man give in exchange for his soul?" (Mark 8:36,37)

Glossary

Adjusted Balance Method–A method for calculating the finance charges on a credit account. It is based on the balance that remains after adjustments are made for credits and payments during the billing cycle.

Adjustable Rate–An interest rate that may change periodically.

Adjustable-Rate Mortgage (ARM)–A mortgage with a rate that may increase or decrease periodically. The rates on these mortgages are usually connected to the prime rate, Treasury Bill rate, or another financial index.

Amortization–The gradual and systematic reduction of debt by application of equal periodic payments. Such payments generally must be sufficient to repay current interest due during the repayment period and to repay the entire principal by the time the loan reaches maturity. An **amortization schedule** is a table which shows the amounts of principal and interest due at regular intervals and the corresponding unpaid principal balance at the time each installment payment is made.

Average Daily Balance–The average amount that exists in an account over a certain period of time. It is calculated by adding the daily balances over a certain period of time and dividing by the number of days in that period. The Average Daily Balance Method uses this to determine interest charges on credit accounts.

Average Daily Balance Method–A method for calculating the finance charges on a credit account. It is based on the average balance that existed each day.

Billing Cycle–The period between billings, usually one month. Charges made during this period will appear on your next statement.

Capped Interest Rate–Used in conjunction with adjustable-rate mortgages (ARMs). With a capped interest rate, when rate changes occur at the expected intervals, there are certain limits on how much the rate can increase or decrease at one time (i.e., in one year). Some ARMs also limit how much the interest rate can increase or decrease over the life of the mortgage.

Cash Advance–A cash loan taken out on a credit card. Cash advances generally do not have a grace period, so interest charges begin on the day the cash advance takes place and continue until it is fully repaid. The interest rates on cash advances are generally very high.

Closing–The point at which a property sale is finalized and title is transferred from the seller to the buyer. (Often called settlement.)

Closing Costs–Expenses and fees that are incurred by the seller and/or buyer in a property transaction. These fees and expenses are in addition to the price of the property. Survey fees, appraisal fees, title insurance premiums, attorney fees, and application fees are all examples of closing costs.

Collateral–Assets that are used by a borrower to secure a loan. The lender can seize the assets if the borrower defaults on the loan.

Compound Interest–Interest that is calculated on the initial principal plus the accumulated (accrued) interest of previous periods.

Consumer Credit/Debt–Non-tax-deductible debt incurred primarily for the purchase of consumer goods and not for a mortgage.

Credit–An agreement or contract in which a borrower receives money or property now and agrees to repay the lender at some point in the future.

Credit Bureau–Any agency that compiles and sells information about the creditworthiness of individuals. These credit bureaus sell the information to potential lenders who use the information to decide whether or not to loan the applicant money or open a credit line. The credit bureau does not make any decisions about who gets credit.

Credit Card–A card that may be used to repeatedly buy products, pay for services, or borrow money on credit.

Credit Rating–A ranking that is based on the detailed financial analysis of a person's financial history and ability to repay debt obligations. This analysis is completed by a credit bureau. Lenders use this rating to decide whether or not to approve a loan or a request for credit.

Credit Score–A measure of credit risk that is calculated from a credit report. A standardized formula is used in the calculation of a credit score. A credit score can be harmed by unfavorable credit card use, making payments late, not having sufficient credit references, judgments and liens, and other factors. Lenders will refer to this credit score when they are underwriting a loan and will often use it to determine what interest rate to charge.

Default–A failure to meet the repayment obligations of a loan or credit agreement. A default on an auto loan or mortgage may result in repossession or foreclosure. A default on credit cards or consumer credit loans may result in judgments or liens.

Due Date–The date by which your payment must be received. On credit card accounts, you must pay your entire balance by this date in order to avoid finance charges. Be aware of the terms of your accounts. Some companies require the payment to be received by a certain time in order to be credited on that business day (i.e., 2pm EST). If your payment is received after the cut-off time, it is considered late. Pay early to avoid late fees and increased interest rates caused by late payments.

Escrow Account–Funds included in the monthly mortgage payment to accumulate the amounts necessary for the future payment of insurance premiums, property taxes, and other items, such as private mortgage insurance (PMI).

Fixed Rate–An interest rate that remains the same and does not increase or decrease with the prime rate or another index.

Fixed-Rate Mortgage or Loan–A mortgage or loan in which the interest rate remains the same for the entire term of the loan.

Grace Period–On credit accounts, the grace period is the period of time during which no interest is charged on new purchases. This usually consists of the number of days between the end of the billing cycle and the due date. It is important to understand that the grace period *is not* a period of time *after* your due date.

If you do not pay the entire "New Balance" by your due date (next statement closing date), finance charges will accrue on new purchases and existing outstanding balances beginning on the first day of your next billing period (i.e., the day after your due date). Example: If your billing cycle ends on May 31 and the due date shown on your statement is June 30 (which will be your next statement closing date), then your grace period is the 30 days between the two dates.

If you pay the balance in full, no interest is charged. However, *if you pay only the minimum monthly payment due*, then you will begin to incur finance charges on your outstanding balance. *Any purchases you make from that point forward will begin to incur interest charges immediately.*

The first time you fail to pay your entire "New Balance," you forfeit your grace period on new purchases until you pay any outstanding balance in full. This is one reason why it is very important to pay your entire balance each month.

On a mortgage, you may be given 15 days after the due date before you are assessed a late fee; but this is not free. You are paying additional interest each day that you are overdue.

Installment Loan–Generally, a loan that is repaid by making a specified number of periodic equal payments. However, some use this term to refer to any consumer credit loan that requires periodic monthly payments, regardless of whether or not the payments are equal or the period is specified.

Interest–The fee that a lender charges to a borrower in exchange for the use of borrowed money. This is usually expressed as an annual percentage of the principal (Interest Rate).

Interest Rate Cap–The maximum interest rate you can be charged on a credit account as determined by your credit agreement. (i.e., variable-rate credit cards, revolving credit accounts, etc.)

Mortgage–A loan that is used to finance a real estate purchase. The borrower gives the lender a lien on the property as collateral for the loan. Interest paid is usually tax deductible.

Past-due Balance Method–A method for calculating interest charges on a credit account in which no interest is charged if the balance is paid in full within a certain period of time.

Points–Finance charges that may be paid by the borrower at the beginning of a mortgage. One point equals 1% of the loan amount. Sometimes borrowers are permitted to buy "discount points" to reduce the interest rate on their mortgage. Points must be paid at closing and are often associated with "closing costs."

Previous Balance Method–A method for calculating interest charges on a credit account that takes the outstanding balance at the conclusion of the previous billing cycle and applies the interest rate to that balance. Under this method, charges incurred in the current billing period are not included.

Principal–The amount of debt remaining on a loan, not including any interest that may have accumulated. The principal is the actual money that you borrowed from the lender; interest is added to the principal.

Private Mortgage Insurance (PMI)–Mortgage insurance that is provided by non-government insurers to protect a lender against loss if a borrower defaults on a mortgage. PMI is usually required when you have less than 20 percent of the total purchase price for a down payment.

Revolving Line of Credit–An agreement by a lending institution to lend a specified amount to a borrower and allow that amount to be borrowed again once it has been repaid. This is the financing method commonly used for "Same-as-Cash" loans and other consumer credit loans; it is often called **revolving credit.**

Same-as-Cash Loan–A consumer credit loan that provides a specified period during which no interest is added to the principal amount. These periods vary but are usually from ninety days to two years (24 months). If the entire balance of the loan (principal) is repaid before the end of the "free financing period," then you will pay no interest or finance charges. However, if the entire balance is not repaid prior to the end of the free period, then interest is added retroactive to the initial purchase date. In other words, the interest has been deferred but is now added to your remaining balance.

Some of these loans require minimum monthly payments on the outstanding balance during the free financing period. This minimum amount is usually a percentage of the outstanding balance (1-5%). Other loans of this type require no minimum monthly payments during the free period, and you have the option to wait until the end of the period to repay the entire balance. You may also pay off the balance at any time during the period.

If the entire balance is not repaid by the end of the free period, then the deferred interest is added to the remaining balance and you begin making monthly payments. The outstanding balance then incurs additional interest charges each month until it is fully repaid.

Simple Interest–A method of calculating interest where the interest is calculated on the principal only and not compounded on previously earned interest.

Statement Closing Date–The last day of your billing cycle. This generally coincides with the due date on your previous statement.

Stewardship–The management or administration of the property, finances, or affairs of someone else. We are to be good **stewards** over the material things which God has placed in our trust. God owns it all; we are merely stewards over what belongs to Him. We are also to be good stewards over God's work, His gospel, and His affairs in this earth; we will be held accountable by Him.

Term–The length of a loan; the period of time over which a loan is repaid. This may be expressed in days, months, or years.

Tithe–A tenth part (10%) of a person's income consecrated to God.

Unsecured Loan (Note)–A loan that is not backed by collateral but only by the integrity and creditworthiness of the borrower. These loans are also referred to as signature loans and promissory notes. They are the opposite of secured loans. (i.e., home mortgages and auto loans) Generally, you must have exceptional credit history and a relationship with the lender in order to qualify for an unsecured loan because you are not pledging an asset that the lender can repossess if you default.

If you can qualify, an unsecured loan is a good alternative to a high-interest consumer credit loan. Unsecured loans usually utilize the simple interest method.

"Upside Down"–This phrase is commonly used to describe **Negative Equity**, which is when you owe more on something than it is worth. If your existing vehicle's trade-in value is less than you owe on it and you trade it in on a newer vehicle, then you will absorb the negative equity into the new loan. In other words, you will be borrowing more than the new vehicle is worth. You are "upside down" immediately.

This condition is often caused by trading vehicles frequently, paying too much for a vehicle initially, accelerated depreciation, or not paying a substantial down payment when you purchase a new vehicle. If you continually roll negative equity into loans on newer vehicles, you will eventually reach a point where you have too much negative equity to qualify for a new loan. When you reach that point, you will have to continue paying off your existing loan or provide a substantial down payment to eliminate some or all of your negative equity.

Index

A

B

H-I

J-L

Notes